OVIA
Regum
bita qua con
amiro prat
u et a S.R.I.
occupata
656

Arx Regia Templum Temp S. Iohannis Templum et Colleg Curia Turris Marescalli Templum et Coenobium S. Bennen Temp Templ S. Maria Suburbium deuastatum
Monachorum Augustin Iesuitarum Dominicanorum Carnentium
I.S. Georgi

Mons Fort

F L U V I U S

E. Dahlbergh
delin.

WARSAW

WARSAW 1998

CONTENTS

TRANSLATION: ROBERT STRYBEL

PRINTED AND BOUND BY S.A., TEL. (58) 302-64-41

PHOTOGRAPHS FROM THE PHOTO LIBRARY OF STANISŁAWA, KRZYSZTOF AND RAFAŁ JABŁOŃSKI TEL: (0-22) 42-27-72

PUBLISHING HOUSE FESTINA S. c. WARSAW 02-908, UL. SOBOLEWSKA 18A, TEL/FAX 42-54-53

ISBN 83-909878-0-5

WARSAW

PHOTOGRAPHY: RAFAŁ JABŁOŃSKI
TEXT: LECH KRZYŻANOWSKI

FESTINA

Main Railway Station

Tomb of the Unknown Soldier

The Royal Castle

Palace of Culture and Science

Old Town Marketplace

Wilanów Palace

Łazienki Palace

ANDERSA

BONIFRATERSKA

Old Town
Marketplace

RYNEK
STAREGO
MIASTA

WYBRZEŻE GDAŃSKIE

The Royal
Castle

PLAC
ZAMKOWY

MOST ŚLĄSKO-DĄBROWSKI

WYBRZEŻE SZCZECIŃSKIE

NOWOLIPKI

AL. SOLIDARNOŚCI

SENATORSKA

WYBRZEŻE KOŚCIUSZKOWSKIE

KRAKOWSKIE PRZEDMIEŚCIE

KAROWA

Tomb of
the Unknown
Soldier

KRÓLEWSKA

MOST SYRENY

AL. JANA PAWŁA II

ŚWIĘTOKRZYSKA

NOWY ŚWIAT

TAMKA

MOST PONIATOWSKIEGO

LUDNA

Palace of
Culture and
Science

KSIĄŻĘCA

ROZBRAT

Main Railway
Station

AL. JEROZOLIMSKIE

MARSZAŁKOWSKA

SOLEC

CHAŁUBIŃSKIEGO

KOSZYKOWA

PIĘKNA

AL. UJAZDOWSKIE

TRASA ŁAZIENKOWSKA

Łazienki Palace

Wilanów Palace
↓

INTRODUCTION

Round the close of the 12th century and the dawn of the 13th, in what is now Warsaw's Mariensztat quarter stood the village of Warszowa. It had been named after Warsz, a popular forename in the knightly Rawicz-Niedźwiad line. When a town was officially established there on a tall escarpment overlooking the Vistula a century later, it was given a name familiar to generations: Warszowa.. As late as the 17th century the term Warszowa was still being used.

Masovia, an area situated along the drainage-basin of the middle Vistula, already in the 10th century had had ties with the Polanian state centred round Gniezno to the west, and subsequently with the Piast dynasty of Kraków. The province's principal town was Płock, the seat of the ruling duke as well as a bishopric. It was not until after the death of Duke Konrad I of Masovia in 1247, that the duchy was divided into the duchies of Płock and Czersk. The reunification of the Duchy of Masovia under Bolesław II (1294) was soon to lead to the formal chartering of the towns of Warszowa, Płock and Rawa. Most likely it was in the early 14th century that the boundaries of today's Old Town were drawn up. An extant note dating from 1313 mentions a ducal castle standing there.

The municipality was granted self-government under the Charter Law of Chełmno. It was not until 1609 that the Old Warsaw Council acquired the hereditary office of chief judge of the court bench. Brick defensive walls, whose thickness was eventually doubled, enclosed a town with an area of 8.5 hectares. The parish church of St John the Baptist was elevated to the rank of a collegiate in 1402. Many other churches were founded, adding splendour to the town.

Castle Square, reproduction of a painting by M. Zalewski.

The fact that the town was situated atop a high escarpment ensured protection against floods and also made it possible to oversee trade routes. In c. 1400 New Town was chartered to the north of Old Town and the Parish of the Blessed Virgin was established. The inhabitants of both towns prospered through trade, crafts and farming. They led peaceful lives round the brick Great House of the ducal castle.

In 1526, the last male heir of the Masovian ducal line died. King Zygmunt the Jagiellonian came from Kraków and spent a month there to oversee the incorporation of his Masovian fiefdom into his kingdom. Warsaw eventually became a royal city. The 1569 Union of Lublin created an integral union between the Polish and Lithuanian states. In 1573, a joint body of deputies selected Warsaw as the venue of the Polish-Lithuanian Sejm (assembly). The death of the last ruler of the House of Jagiełło expanded the role of the general sejms to include the election of Polish monarchs. In 1596, Warsaw became the royal residence, entailing the transfer of offices associated with the king and the Commonwealth. The process of moving the royal court from Kraków to Warsaw lasted until 1611. Warsaw's population grew from 6,000 in the mid-16th century to some 10,000 before the century was out.

Only in fairy tales can Cinderella turn into a beautiful princess in the twinkling of an eye. But the process of transforming Warsaw into a royal capital lasted from 1598 to 1619, for that is how long it took to build a new royal residence. It annexed the old Great House of the Dukes of Masovia. King Zygmunt III Vasa had the town surrounded by earthen ramparts (1621-1626), thereby increasing its area to 126 hectares. The extensive new land between the mediaeval town and the ramparts were given over the agricultural pursuits and sparsely built up with typically suburban structures.

King Władysław IV, the son of Zygmunt III Vasa, issued a separate decree at his coronation sejm saying: 'Our town of Old Warsaw has become famous as the residence first of Their Highnesses the Dukes of Masovia, whose splendid mausolea have graced it ever since, then of His late Majesty Zygmunt August and Anna Jagiellonian, and for quite some time of our late Parent; also because of the triumphs achieved and trophies captured in Moscow, from the Turks and Tartars, that it rightfully ranks among the most illustrious of towns and as the venue of sejms is hereby enshrined in public law.' From 1570 to 1655 Warsaw was the scene of 65 sejms and six elections.

Up to 70,000 people participated in the above-mentioned election of Władysław IV. To display the power of their houses, some aristocrats arrived with military escorts of up to 1,000 troops. All townsfolk were obliged to give up their lodgings to the guests. No less troublesome were the throngs occupying suburban inns. For the town's permanent inhabitants, elections involved more hardships than profits.

The considerable number of churches, palaces and manorhouses gracing Krakowskie Przedmieście added splendour to the Warsaw of the Vasa years. Many of them had been erected by outstanding architects and builders. Among the extant monuments are the King Zygmunt Column, funded by Władysław IV, and Kazimierz Palace, but most of the buildings were destroyed after the Swedes captured Warsaw in 1655-1656. The town panoramas sketched and painted before the 'deluge' (as Poland's Nobel Prize-winning novelist Henryk Sienkiewicz called the Swedish invasion) reveal an impressive wealth of monumental structures. Jean de Laboreur, the secretary of the French Embassy, thus described his impressions after visiting the Royal Palace, later known as Kazimierz Palace: 'Italy, which we were to later see, has nothing so splendid nor truly lordly. I must admit I was charmed and felt as if I were being transported in a dream to some sorcerer's palace...' The greatness of the Commonwealth was expressed not only by the modernised Royal Castle but also by the palaces of Adam Kazanowski, Jerzy Ossoliński, the Miniszechs, Radziwiłłs and many others, known from descriptions and drawings. The latter half of the 17th century was conducive to the rebuilding of the town and the growth of its population. In 1659 it counted a mere 6,000 inhabitants, but when royal architect Tylman of Gameren was surveying and recording all the town's real estate at the turn of the 17th to 18th centuries, 18,000 people were found living in Warsaw. A considerable share of those inhabitants lived in so-called jurisdictions or unchartered areas of the town which could develop solely after the whim of their owners. They did

capital. The royal election of 1697 led to the coronation in Kraków of August II Wettin. At the same time, the supporters of French elect Count Conti proclaimed him king. In 1699, an ordinary sejm formally acknowledged the election, but in 1704 the Warsaw Confederation proclaimed the dethronement of August II. Stanisław Leszczynski was elected king and it was not until 1717 that the 'mute sejm' ratified a treaty regulating relations between Poland and Saxony. It was not surprising then that the construction of a residence for the unwanted monarch was planned for outside the town's limits and attached to barracks.

Numerous sketches and alternative versions of projects planned for Warsaw have remained in archives. Permanent evidence of Saxon designs for the panorama of Warsaw are the eastern hull of the Royal Castle, as seen from the Vistula, designed by Gaetano Chiveri, and the partially-preserved Saxon Garden.

The reign of Stanisław August Poniatowski (1764-95) and the final years of independent, pre-partition Poland brought with them significant changes. The town's population had considerably exceeded 100,000. The Boni Ordinis (Good Order) Commission developed a new town charter, although its legali-

Panorama of Warsaw by Dahlberg, 1656.

not pay any taxes to the town treasury. A proposed tax to finance a sewer system and cobbled roads met with such nagry protests from the gentry -- that they were exempted from paying. The problem of Warsaw's road surfaces is an old one indeed.

Streets such as Miodowa, Długa and Krakowskie Przedmieście in the near proximity of the Royal Castle developed rather quickly following the mid-17th century. New religious structures were erected. The traditional directions of development continued: southward to Wilanów, westward to Wola and northward to Bielany. An important role was played in all this by above-mentioned architect Tylman of Gameren, whose major achievements have survived. The summer palace at Wilanów remains a lasting memento of the artistic patronage of King John III Sobieski, Poland's last great monarch.

The following 50 years were not propitious ones for Poland's

sation had to wait until the revolutionary Four-year Sejm convened in 1791. The town was endowed with administrative and judicial authority, its jurisdictions were abolished and their area were divided up into administrative districts. The entirety was surrounded by earthen ramparts which enclosed an area of 1,500 hectares. The king himself as well as aristocratic houses close to him provided funds for the town's development. The urban landscape was enriched by such architects as Jakub Fontana, Dominik Merlini, Szymon Bogumił Zug and others.

Following the third and last partition of Poland, Warsaw ceased being a centre of government decision-making. Some of the inhabitants left, especially those connected with the former royal court and state officialdom. The Duchy of Warsaw (1807-1815), a truncated semi-autonomous state set up by Napoléon, maintained the town's developmental tendencies, and the

Old Town Marketplace. View of the Dekert and Barss frontages with the Mermaid Fountain. A 1922 photograph by Poddębski.

Kingdom of Poland period witnessed the creation of Warsaw's Castle Square, Theatre Square, Bank Square and Three Crosses Square. Nowy Świat Street received a roughly uniform architectural shape, and Aleje Jerozolimskie -- the town's main east-west artery -- was delineated. In addition to dozens of public buildings such as the Royal University of Warsaw (1816), the Polytechnical Preparatory School (1826) and the Office of Building, more than 400 new townhouses were built. Antoni Corazzi (1820-1825) built the seat of the Society of Friends of Learning, in front of which the Copernicus Monument of Bertel Thorwaldsen was erected (1830).

After the November Insurrection had been crushed (1831), the Russian partitioners turned Warsaw into a provincial capital. The liquidation of the university began, and some Catholic churches were transformed into Russian Orthodox places of worship. Along the town's northern fringes the construction of a fortified citadel complex got under way (1832), and a 1,300-metre esplanade was marked out round its periphery. The population of Warsaw dropped to 114,000.

The first steel bridge spanning the River Vistula was built by Stanisław Kierbedź in 1860-1864. The Warsaw-Vienna Railway was established in 1839-1848 and the St Petersburg Railway -- in 1862. The elimination of tariff barriers with Russia spurred the dramatic growth of international trade, industry and technology. Towards the end of the 19th century Warsaw's population was approaching 900,000. From 1883, the city's expansion was accompanied by the construction of the Lindley water-supply and sewer network. Warsaw's electrification was started in 1902. Such gifted architects as Henryk and WŁadysŁaw Marconi, Franciszek Maria Lanci, Alfons Kropiwnicki, Jan Gay and their many skilled colleagues erected a number of splendid edifices, including hotels, banks, credit societies and palaces. Warsaw was becoming an important metropolis.

Warsaw began taking over the functions of a capital even before Poland regained its Independnece in 1918. From 1916 there functioned a Temporary Council of State and subsequently the Regency Council of the Kingdom of Poland. A Warsaw Capital City Council came into being. In 1916 Tadeusz Tołwiński's team came up with a 'Preliminary Sketch of Plan to Regulate Warsaw'. The people of Warsaw and the municipal authorities were ready for the return of independence and determined to defend it. Already in 1920 that opportunity presented itself.

During the 20-year period between the two World Wars all of Warsaw's access roads were modernised. The railway system was made more efficient by routing rail-lines through walled corridors and tunnels. The city's ecology was improved by creating broad green belts between built-up areas. The northern district of Żoliborz became an example of a model district of housing co-operatives. Academic campuses were developed and ministry buildings and banks were built. 'Functional Warsaw', a plan developed by Jan Chmielewski and Szymon Syrkus, mapped out the directions of further research and development but was cut short by the outbreak of the Second World War in 1939.

At that time, Warsaw covered an area of 134.7 square kilometres, and its population stood at 1,289,500 (as against 758,400 in 1918). In September 1939 12% of Warsaw was destroyed, and the destruction of the Warsaw Ghetto in 1943 increased the losses by another 12%. The 1944 Warsaw Uprising increased the destruction by 28% and by January 1945, as a result of systematic destruction by the Germans, it grew by more than 30%. About 700,000 of the city's permanent inhabitants lost their lives.

Immediately after the liberation of Warsaw on 17 January 1945, the government adopted a resolution proclaiming Warsaw the capital of Poland and set up a Bureau for Reconstruction. Several weeks later, the Capital City Reconstruction Bureau was established, which had all the necessary empowerment. Decrees on the reconstruction of Warsaw and the communalisation of all its land made practical activities possible. The author has invoked history and has presented the motives and manner of the operations launched after 1945. In his 1996 book, architect Czesław Bielecki accurately and concisely characterised the subject of our album: 'Warsaw is a city-place-name which is reborn in the imagination and in symbols.' It is worth familiarising oneself with the mechanism of that phenomenon.

The East-West Route.

Tourist choo-choo train.

CASTLE SQUARE

This place is at once symbolic and magical. It is here that history had a rendez-vous with the future. Nearly everything one sees round this spot has been built since 1945. It is uncertain whether Konrad II Duke of Czersk or his brother Bolesław II had ever intended to set up a town and mark off the site of their castle in this once uninhabited portion of the Warsaw escarpment. In 1313 a document confirmed the existence of the town and ducal court. Everything, of course, looked quite different back then. Near this spot was the main road leading into the ducal castle-town of Warszowa. Thanks to its development into a bustling urban centre, the parliament of Poland and Lithuania, which united in 1569, later chose Warsaw as the venue of a common parliament and of royal elections (1573). To this day, Zygmunt III Vasa surveys Warsaw's Old Town from atop his obelisk-like column. It was he who had moved his permanent residence there from Kraków, initiating the city's rise to capital status. When the column came crashing to the ground in January 1945, the name 'Warsaw' was little more than a geographic or historical concept. But on 17 January the government proclaimed it would continue to be the capital and would get rebuilt.

The green areas round the base of the defensive walls mark the place where the town's former moats had been. The ruined houses on that side of Podwale Street were not rebuilt in order to provide Old Town residents with better living conditions. That had also been the aim of the East-West Thoroughfare

(1949), popularly known as the W-Z Route, which channelled transit traffic through a tunnel. That concept had been developed in 1942, when everything in the vicinity, save for the Royal Castle, was still intact. Already back then, as the Second World War was raging, monument conservators were seeking new solutions.

A horse-drawn carriage in Castle Square.

ROYAL CASTLE

In 1526, Zygmunt Jagiellonian the Old spent a month at the then ducal castle of Warsaw -- a fiefdom being absorbed into the Kingdom of Poland together with all of Masovia following the heirless death of its last duke. From 1569 to 1571 the castle was significantly expanded for his son who was overseeing preparations for Poland's merger with Lithuania. A fire at Royal Wawel Castle in Kraków (1595) accelerated the transfer of the seat of Zygmunt III to Warsaw. From there it was closer not only to Wilno, the Lithuanian capital, but also to Stockholm. As the son of Sweden's Jan III Vasa and Polish Princess Anna Jagiellonian, the Polish monarch had dreams of obtaining the Swedish crown. The actual construction lasted from 1598 to 1619 and created a five-winged hull at the escarpment's edge. The building's façade, as seen from Castle Square, has retained the appearance it had back then. The Zygmunt clock tower was named after the monarch. The Władysław Tower is the corner one in the courtyard. The kings of Saxony's Wettin Dynasty had the wing on the Vistula side built according to a 1737 design by Gaetano Chiaveri.

Stanisław August Poniatowski, the last king of Poland (1764-1795), with the aid of a team of gifted architects, rebuilt much of the castle's interior. The Ball-Room, projecting inward from the Vistula side (1771-1781) after a design by court architects Dominik Merlini and Chrystian Kamsetzer, was an outstanding achievement. Also magnificent were the royal chambers en suite in the south wing. Following more than half a century of stagnation, the monarch carried out essential changes in the building's interior. He restored to it a symbolic character befitting the Polish Kingdom's ruling house.

As a result of the alterations, a gallery of Polish kings was set up in the Marble Room (1796-1771). The Senatorial Anteroom became the Knights' Chamber (1781-1786) which sang the praises of Poland's military prowess through the paintings and portraits of Marcello Bacciarelli. Sculpted portraits of famous Poles rounded out that national pantheon. The décor of the Senatorial Chamber, reconstructed according to a design by Zachariasz Longuelune (1740(, alludes to the promulgation of the Third of May Constitution, Europe's first written constitution. Although the constitution was overturned a year later by Russian interference and the Confederation of Targowica, Warsaw's Royal Castle became a lasting national symbol thanks to its political and artistic stature. The evaluation of the role played by the last Polish king continues to divide Poles who traditionally have espoused divergent political viewpoints. The symbolism embodied by the Castle itself, however, is beyond discussion.

From 1795 to 1831 various administrations had held office in the Castle. Following the fall of the November Insurrection, it became the seat of tsarist viceroys. In 1818-1821 as number of buildings in front of the castle's façade were taken down, thus creating Castle Square. The viceroys sought to efface the

< A misty morning in Castle Square.

national and patriotic character of the interior. For instance, the appointments of the Marble Room were removed (1835), Canaletto's paintings were taken to Russia (1832), and the Hall of Deputies and Senate Hall were liquidated. The elevations were redone. In 1915, the Monument Preservation Society began compiling photographic documentation of the building's interior, and conservation efforts soon got under way. While restoring the courtyard, architect Kazimierz Skórewicz uncovered the mediaeval elevation of the Great House, a fragment of the castle of the Dukes of Masovia.

After Poland regained its independence (1918), the Castle became the foremost edifice of the Second Republic and the presidential residence (1926). Poland's independence and sovereignty, restored after 123 years, again united Poles who had lived in three different partition zones separated from each other by borders. As legal systems were unified and a uniform educa-

Portal of Władysław Tower.

tional system in the Polish language was developed, propagation of national symbols -- everywhere from nurseries to restored Polish academic institutions -- became an important element of national education. That facilitated making people aware of the fact that Poland was the common homeland and state of citizens from all three partitions.

Warsaw's Royal Castle, where the diplomatic corps met the President of Poland and assemblies of state rank were held, played an important role in Poland's collective imagination. A Batory and Rejtan Hall was established. In it were displayed the paintings of charismatic artist Jan Matejko, whose historical themes helped to preserve Poland's national identity in the latter half of the 19th century.

The Castle was damaged during the siege of Warsaw in September 1939, and on 17 September it became engulfed in flames, causing part of its roof to collapse.

The evacuation of its most valuable treasures had begun the moment the war broke out. When the Castle's fate became a foregone conclusion, teams of specialists removed and disassembled doors, portals, fire-places, furniture, wainscoting, fragments of stuccowork, etc. Volunteers from Old Town also helped in the evacuation of the Castle's art works and furnishings. The evacuation effort continued the end of 1939, when German sappers prepared to blow up what was left of the Castle and made the area out of bounds to Poles. Microfilms documenting these activities were soon in the hands of the Polish Government-in-Exile in London. The Castle's ruins were blown up in autumn 1944.

In 1947, the ruins were cleared of rubble, and all reusable ele-

East Elevation.

Ball-room.

ments were carefully preserved. In 1949, the sejm adopted a resolution calling for the reconstruction of the Royal Castle, but the state and Communist Party authorities were opposed to restoring this symbol of state sovereignty. After more than 20 years, in 1971 the authorities succumbed to the unmitigating efforts of citizens and various organisations. Various studies, historical and archaeological research as well as cataloguing had gone on since 1947, but now a civic committee for the reconstruction was established. It was decided to finance the project through free-will donations. And so the nation rebuilt its Royal Castle, joined by émigré Poles abroad. An appeal directed to all Poles in 1971 recalled the Castle's symbolism and called for its reconstruction through the common efforts of society. Citizens' committees arose in nearly every locality and collected funds and accepted gifts in kind. In Castle Square, a huge glass-encased collection box was set out, and everyone could watch it fill up with Polish and foreign currency as well as wedding rings, brooches and other 'gifts of the heart', as they were called. Today, when we restore our sense of social ties by helping the victims of the 1997 flood or donating to charitable causes, such an attitude seems completely normal. But back then, the Castle-reconstruction drive was the first such spontaneous, grass-roots campaign in many years. Since 1980, the Royal Castle of Warsaw has functioned as a museum-like institution. In 1989, its final fragment, the Ball-Room, was opened to the public.

To the question 'What is the Royal Castle to Poles today?' -- one must reply: a symbol of the national continuation of state sovereignty. When aerial bombardment set the Royal Castle ablaze on 17 September 1939, Warsovians did not know that on the outskirts of the besieged city Adolf Hitler, Chancellor of the Third Reich, was watching the smoke billowing up from central Warsaw and posing for photographs. They did know, however, that that morning the Soviet army had attacked their homeland. That was the reason for the determination with which they carried away and concealed every fragment of the Castle they could. The retreating German army blew up the ruins after the city's inhabitants had been driven out in autumn 1944. For that reason, Stanisław Lorentz, director of the National Museum in Warsaw, was not alone in constantly calling for reconstruction of the Castle but enjoyed grass-roots support.

Architect Jan Zachwatowicz headed the civic commission

Statue of Chronos in Knights' Hall. >

The Marble Room.

which programmed the reconstruction effort, approved all technical sketches and supervised the quality of the work being carried out. To his authority and determination the edifice owes so much of the masonry, stuccowork and carved-wood elements which returned to their former place. This was a new building but it had remained faithful to its prototype. Its individual elements were new, although the surviving original fragments woven into them can clearly be seen by visitors in the building's façades and interiors. And no-one can question the authenticity of a ground-floor stretch of wall in the Great House of the Dukes of Masovia. A surprising series of regular openings drilled in the brick wall were meant for explosives. It should also be added that the castle has been fitted with more than a dozen different modern systems to ensure its efficient functioning.

After reconstruction got under way, a survey was conducted as to what functions the rebuilt Castle should perform. The dominant view was that its historic halls should be restored to serve as a museum. But most respondents also felt it should be open to the public for concerts and the commemorative assemblies of civic organisations. The Castle was seen as the venue of

award presentations and meetings with outstanding personalities. And indeed, the Castle has been performing all those functions. Work is continuing on preparation of the so-called Kubicki Arcade (19th century) on the Vistula side for public viewing as well as the landscaping of green areas which will serve as the former royal gardens.

The Throne Room.

< *Conference room.*

THE ZYGMUNT COLUMN

This monument was erected by Władysław IV in honour of his father, Zygmunt III Vasa. Augustyn Locci developed the concept of its spatial setting, and royal architect Konstanty Tencalla designed the monument. Clemente Molli created a model of the statue, and the figure was cast by Daniel Tym. In 1644, the statue of King Zygmunt took its place atop the column at the head of Krakowskie Przedmieście Street. It could be seen from Senatorska Street as it stood in a modest square before Kraków Gate. Crests and a foundation inscription adorned its socle.

The king had thus become a Warsovian, 'one of us'. He also made his way into poems and songs. Stefan Wiechecki, the bard of Warsaw's démi-monde, in his newspaper column once wrote about a slyboots who had sold the monument to an unsuspecting bumpkin. 'Tell us, King Zygmunt, do tell us pray, was Warsaw ever as beautiful as it is today?' a 1950s song in waltz tempo asked. But back in January 1945, a short while before Warsaw was liberated, the Column was blown up. Upon crashing to the ground, King Zygmunt lost an arm and foot, but otherwise survived. Art conservators took good care of the monarch. Builders brought a granite column from Strzegom, but it could not be set up at exactly the same spot it had been before. The road surface had been altered in connection with the building of the East-West Route -- a fact not lost on streetwise Warsovians. In 1949, poet Władysław Broniewski came up with the following verse:

'King Zygmunt, have you been set up nice and proper up there on high?

I stand and that should suffice,

My sword counts the centuries going by.'

METAL-ROOFED PALACE

Situated on the Vistula escarpment beneath the Castle's south-eastern corner, this building is an interesting, albeit seldom-visited Warsaw monument. The history of this Baroque structure began in 1651. In 1655 it was devastated during the Swedish siege, in 1698 it was rented to Jerzy Dominik Lubomirski, a prominent aristocrat who became the royal chamberlain in 1702. In 1720 he purchased the structure, reconstructed it and built on a south wing, giving the building the appearance we know today. In 1772 the building was purchased by King Stanisław August Poniatowski to serve as quarters for royal-court officials and courtiers. Józef Poniatowski, who was to become commander-in-chief of the army of the Duchy of Warsaw and participated in the Napoleonic wars as the Grande Armée's only Polish marshal, became lord of the manor.

The palace was partially destroyed by a blaze in 1944, and was painstakingly restored according to a painting by Bernardo Bellotto. The king had ordered a set of townscapes from his favourite artist. They made it possible to recreate many of Warsaw's architectural monuments. The appointments for the rooms of the north wing, designed by Dominik Merlini (1778-1780), have fortunately survived. The stuccowork was the work of Antoni Bianchi, and the carpentry and woodwork is attributed to Johann Jacobs (1778-1780). Since 1988 the palace has been part of the Royal Castle complex and houses, among other things, an outstanding gallery of Oriental rugs.

< Interior of the Chapel.

OLD TOWN

The sacred reliquary of Warsaw -- Old Town,
With the mould and mist of centuries all round.
Like a pensive oldster, tall and strong who
His grandchildren's cradle does lovingly view.

Artur Oppman (1867-1931), a resident of the house at 8 Kanonia Street, thus began one of his numerous poems devoted to this beloved, symbolic place. Printed in many collections and periodicals, they tied the heart-strings of all Warsaw to Oldie (Starówka), as the historic town-centre is popularly called.

Built in the 14th century to serve the needs of Masovia, it covered an area of 8.5 hectares including the Castle. The main road across Castle Square led down Świętojańska Street, the Marketplace and Nowomiejska Street, whence one could enter New Town through the barbican. Save for a few minor modifications, the arrangement and dimensions of its streets have not changed, and the building parcels have remained as narrow as ever. In the 18th and 19th centuries the buildings were elevated and the land between streets was built up. The major changes of the royal capital took place beyond the confines of Old Town.

Brzozowa Street.

After 1918, restoration efforts were launched to improve the appearance of the then impoverished quarter. The defensive walls were exposed. The narrow streets, numerous passageways between houses, annexes and cellars fostered neighbourly contacts and were a boon to freedom-fighters during the period of partitions, in World War Two and also after martial law was declared on 13 December 1981.

Ninety percent of Old Town was destroyed during the 1944 Warsaw Uprising. But the underground zone of mediaeval and later cellars beneath each building had remained intact. In force during post-war re-

Backstreet

construction was the principle that every usable façade or wall fragment should be put to use. But to local residents and visitors alike, the original elements, often hidden from view by post-war plaster, are not the main thing. What really counts is the preserved character and atmosphere of this place, even though annexes deeply set back into the courtyards were not rebuilt in order to improve living conditions by decreasing congestion.

Piwna Street.

Wąski Dunaj Street.

WARSAW ARCHICATHEDRAL

The Warsaw parish commemorating the Decapitation of St John the Baptist is as old as the town itself. Its first rector was mentioned in a document dating from 1321. Janusz I the Elder, Duke of Masovia, brought his canons there from his castle chapel in Czersk. In 1406, the Bishop of Gniezno confirmed the erection of a collegiate. There too the last king of Poland swore in the Constitution of the 3rd of May 1791. After Poland had lost its independence, the collegiate was elevated to the rank of the Warsaw bishopric, and in 1817 it was proclaimed an archcathedral. In the Catholic Church the archbishop of Warsaw is the primate of Poland, and that grants him primacy over other bishops as well as the chairmanship of the Episcopate Conference

The gothic hull of the brick church came into being in several phases in the 14th century, and reconstruction was continued on into the 15th century in order to complete an extremely tall tower. A number of chapels were built on to the south nave. The roof of the cathedral was consumed in a blaze in 1939. Following heavy fighting during the Warsaw Uprising, the entire building, together with the neighbouring Jesuit Church, was blown up. It was rebuilt in 1947-1956 under the supervision of the Primate's Council for Church Reconstruction according to a design by Jan Zachwatowicz. Although contemporary in character, the Świetojańska Street façade alludes to gothic tradition.

Splendid works of art fell victim to combat and planned destruction after the uprising. The stalls in the presbytery, a votive offering of King John III Sobieski for his victory in the Battle of Vienna (1683), as well as the choir loft funded by King Jan Kazimierz c. 1560, have been recreated. A marble tomb slab of the last Dukes of Masovia, Stanisław and Janusz, a fragment of a monument funded by Princess Anna and King Zygmunt III, and a typically Renaissance tombstone of a Polish knight (c. 1530, south nave) are all that survived. The chapel of Primate Stefan Wyszyński, known as the Primate of the Millennium, adjoins the north nave. Numerous contemporary epitaphs on the walls are evidence of the patriotic sentiments of the faithful who, up till 1989, could freely commemorate great Poles and historical events only in the safety of churches.

Old Town Marketplace. >

OLD TOWN MARKETPLACE

Entrance to Fukier House.

Wilczek House.

Moving along Świętojańska Street from Castle Square towards the Marketplace is like walking through history. Along this route on 3 May 1791 deputies and senators moved in a patriotic procession carrying King Stanisław August Poniatowski shoulder-high, so that he might swear in the first modern constitution of the collapsing Commonwealth.

Along this route in 1995, in deep reflection they accompanied the mortal remains of the last monarch which were to be enshrined in the archcathedral's crypts. On 11 November, from its naves emerged patriots -- also during martial law -- to mark Independence Day, not recognised by the authorities, and lay flowers at the Tomb of the Unknown Soldier. Waving Solidarity placards, demonstrators once began their marches in this street to demand the release of internees, only to find themselves face to face with police detachments in full riot gear. The generation that rebuilt this quarter has long been retired. Everything has become normal.

A painter in the Marketplace.

But in this town, memories do not fade.

From a typical residential quarter, which was rebuilt as such (the dedication ceremony took place in 1953), Old Town has evolved into an international tourist attraction. In 1981, together with the Royal Way (Krakowskie Przedmieście and Nowy Świat up to Aleje Jerozolimskie), it was entered on UNESCO's world heritage list. At the same session, the international body included on its list the historic centre of Rome. In Warsaw's case, UNESCO was mainly giving recognition to the manner in which relics of historical heritage had been preserved, the way the destroyed had been recreated and a normal, vibrant, urban fabric had been created.

The size of the Old Town Marketplace, whose dimensions are 73 × 90 metres, is in proportion to the size of the streets and individual building plots. Towards the end of the 15th century

there were 150 of the latter. The initial impression one gets when scanning the Marketplace is the relatively small size of the individual houses, their nearly standardised three-window width and the clearly built-up roof area. That build-up took place mainly in the 18th and 19th centuries as a result of the town's population growth. Today's impression of the Marketplace as a congested area is the result of growing tourism, although on weekends Warsovians account for some of the crowds. For them, Old Town remains a favourite place for leisurely strolls. In 1915, each side of the Marketplace was given its own name.

The patron of the main road to New Town was Father Hugo Kołątaj (1750-1812), a philosopher and politician who had been instrumental in preparing the Third of May Constituion as well

as urban reform. He spent his final years at No. 19, Wójtowska House, the only one with a balcony in that Marketplace frontage. Jan Dekert (1738-1790), a merchant and mayor of Warsaw, who led a struggle for burgher rights, is the patron of the side encompassing the Warsaw Historical Museum.

The buildings there suffered the least destruction in 1944, because they had undergone thorough repairs and restoration before 1939. The opposite side is dedicated to Ignacy Zakrzewski-Wyssogota, the first elected mayor of Warsaw (1792), who made an important contribution to the Kościuszko Insurrection (1794).

The side named after Franciszek Barss (1760-1812), another outstanding citizen, closes off the Marketplace from the east. By 1945, only the ground-floor stretch of this frontage had survived. Although plans to reconstruct these buildings had been drawn up, the authorities decided against it. They wanted to leave this side open to provide a scenic view of the Vistula. Ultimately, however, the Franciszek

Simonettich House.

Barss side was also rebuilt.

The reconstruction of the Marketplace had advanced considerably, but the Vistula side was still being kept at zero-level. The management of the reconstruction project all at once ordered teams of masons to brick in all the façades to a height of two metres in a single day. The next morning the high commission was greatly surprised. More importantly, the argument for rebuilding all four sides of the Marketplace became convincing. In this section the Museum of Literature is now housed.

The Zakrzewski Frontage.

JAN KILIŃSKI MONUMENT

THE WARSAW MERMAID

On a simple, granite hexagon stands a master cobbler closely linked to the Jacobins, a leader of the Warsaw townsfolk in the Kościuszko Insurrection (17-18 April 1794). Twice wounded  during the defence of the city, after the insurrection had been crushed Jan Kiliński was imprisoned by the Russians in the Petropavlovsk Fortress in St Petersburg. He served as a town councillor after his release. Sculptor Stanisław Jackowski was the creator of this dynamic figure which, since 1936, has marked the place where Piekarska Street meets Podwale (Along-the-Ramparts) Street. The monument was removed in 1942 and returned in 1959.

From the earliest times, the mermaid had been the heraldic symbol of Warsaw.

Adorning seals and documents, her appearance had changed over the centuries. But always in one hand she held a weapon and in the other -- a shield, always ready to defend her town. Konstanty Hegel created this figure in 1854, and it was cast in the Warsaw factory of Karol Minter. Originally the monument had stood in the Old Town Marketplace, later it was moved, but most likely it will eventually return to its former location.

LITTLE INSURGENT'S MNUMENT

A small youngster in a huge helmet taken from a Germans, armed with a machine-gun, stands on what is left of the bastion of the outer defensive walls where Kiliński Street meets Podwale. In 1946, Jerzy Jarnuszkiewicz had developed a small plaster model. After being enlarged and cast in bronze, it was set up in 1983 to pay tribute to the young participants of the Warsaw Uprising. As couriers, such youngsters carried orders, post and the underground press to the freedom-fighters.

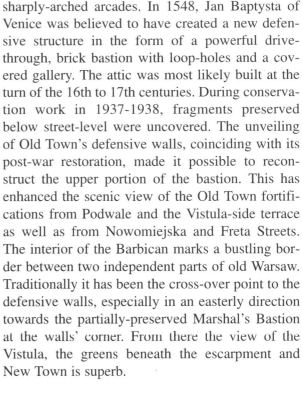

BARBICAN

The moat separating Old Town from New Town was spanned in the 15th century by a bridge, set on sharply-arched arcades. In 1548, Jan Baptysta of Venice was believed to have created a new defensive structure in the form of a powerful drive-through, brick bastion with loop-holes and a covered gallery. The attic was most likely built at the turn of the 16th to 17th centuries. During conservation work in 1937-1938, fragments preserved below street-level were uncovered. The unveiling of Old Town's defensive walls, coinciding with its post-war restoration, made it possible to reconstruct the upper portion of the bastion. This has enhanced the scenic view of the Old Town fortifications from Podwale and the Vistula-side terrace as well as from Nowomiejska and Freta Streets. The interior of the Barbican marks a bustling border between two independent parts of old Warsaw. Traditionally it has been the cross-over point to the defensive walls, especially in an easterly direction towards the partially-preserved Marshal's Bastion at the walls' corner. From there the view of the Vistula, the greens beneath the escarpment and New Town is superb.

Interior of the Barbican.

NEW
TOWN

Originally a suburb situated to the north of Old Town, from the late 14th century New Town began to develop along the road leading to Zakroczym. It led along today's Freta and Zakroczymska Streets. A ducal privilege, granted in 1408, removed the settlement from the jurisdiction of the Old Town mayor and gave it its own self-government. At that time, a town-hall, probably built of wood, was situated in the then rectangular market-place. It was mentioned in 1497. It may be assumed that the entire quarter was built up with wooden structures which were consumed by a big blaze in 1544. Its inhabitants were engaged in crafts and farming. Intensive building got under way in the latter half of the 18th century. With their size and distinct appearance, baroque palaces enhanced the quarter's otherwise modest architecture. The most impressive was the palace of Jan Fryderyk Sapieha at No. 6 Zakroczymska Street. In 1791, New Town lost its independence by being absorbed into the modernised structure of Warsaw. The 1944 destruction amounted to 80% of the buildings reconstructed from 1949 to 1957. The reconstruction projects were drawn up under the direction of Mieczysław Kuzma. He was inspired by the baroque and classicist forms characteristic of the 18th century which differed from the small-scale row-houses of Old Town.

CHURCH OF THE VISITATION
OF THE BVM

Situated on a spit of the escarpment, below which stretches a riverside boulevard rimmed with grassy recreational areas, this church is a characteristic landmark in the townscape of Warsaw's historic district as seen from the Vistula. It is situated in New Town at Przyrynek Street and is the city's earliest historic brick structure beyond the confines of Old Town. It was founded in 1411 for the New Town parish by Janusz the Elder, duke of Masovia, and his wife Anna, and initially had but a single nave. Today's three-nave basilica-like structure was the result of expansion carried out in the latter half of the 16th century. It was then that a tall brick bell-tower was erected. Situated as it was at the edge of the quarter, it had been frequently destroyed during fighting. Although repeatedly restored and rebuilt as a result, it has nevertheless managed to retain its picturesque, gothic qualities.

prioress ended her conversation with their delegation by saying: 'Throughout the 250 years our cloister has been in existence, there has never been a precedent for violating our rule of cloistered isolation. But this moment is so peculiar for Poland, that I agree.'

On 22 August, some 1,000 people died beneath the ruins of the bombed church and cloister, including 35 nuns and four priests.

ST CASIMIR'S CHURCH OF
THE SISTERS OF THE
BLESSED SACRAMENT

This church and cloister are a true gem among the architectural monuments of New Town which has no dearth of historic structures. The buildings and extensive gardens were founded by Queen Maria Kazimiera Sobieska as a votive offering for the victory at Vienna achieved by her husband, King John III Sobieski. Court architect Tylman of Gameren built it as a central church (1688-1692) in a mild baroque style, set on a Greek cross foundation and with a copula. The interior was filled by appointments of high artistic quality, continually enriched by passing generations. The Sisters of the Blessed Sacrament are cloistered nuns. But that did not prevent them from operating a boarding-school for girls entrusted to their care. The fact that not only their characters were shaped is attested to by two of its pupils who went on to become outstanding Polish writers: Eliza Orzeszkowa and Maria Konopnicka.

In August 1944, Home Army fighters of the Warsaw Uprising were desperately searching for premises for their wounded. The

THE ROYAL WAY

The road leading south from Old Town, once known as the Czersk Road, linked two ducal castles. Over the years, the names of various stretches of the road changed. Unofficially, the term Royal Way emerged as a recollection of the splendid processions of the royal entourage in a bygone era.

Data on the destruction suffered by Warsaw in 1939-1944 are reliable. They emerged from a balance-sheet of expert evaluations needed to draw up cost estimates of the restoration and rebuilding programme. One should not forget the directive calling for the incorporation into the new structures of all reusable, surviving fragments of façades and external walls. Not everything had to be built from scratch.

Standing with one's back to the King Zygmunt Column and looking to the buildings on the left one sees an old guardhouse built onto the convent of St Ann's Church. The work of Christian Aigner (1820-1821), it succumbed to a blaze and was rebuilt in 1949. The history of the building next door, now the seat of the Polish Commonwealth Association which fosters ties with Poles world-wide, was similar. Next to it stands the building of charitable societies which incorporates a considerable number of fragments of the former Kazanowski Palace. It includes an early-baroque gallery and portals. On the Mariensztat side there is a plaque on the wall of the palace's bastion proclaiming that here Master Zagłoba (a comic character in Henryk Sienkiewicz's historical 'Trilogy') went into combat against a band of monkeys. The Chapel of the Immaculate Conception, which is entered from the street, was the former palace chapel, rebuilt by CorazCorazzi in 1818.

Towns destroyed by the cruelty of war do not perish irretrievably, since the surviving generation, determined to preserve its heritage, is guided by motives and values stronger than the lunacy of destruction.

The character of Nowy Świat Street, where the destruction was greater, is somewhat different. The post-war authors of its reconstruction did not take the scale of the street into consideration but chose to revert to 19th-century conceptions. But that reconstruction project is now history. When in 1995 it was decided to resurface the street, heated debates erupted as to how the project should be carried out. It is rather nice living in a city where such issues, even when sometimes exaggerated, can still enflame public passions.

A view to the Old Town.

Towards the end of the 18th century, the building's rear elevation from Senatorska Street was done over in the style of the late baroque. It was burnt down in 1944.

After the ruins were catalogued, they were dismantled, with all decorative details carefully preserved. That was necessary while the W-Z Route was being built in a tunnel below. The building's reconstruction was completed to coincide with the opening of the Route in 1949. The façade continues to enchant the beholder with the elegance and finesse of its details and continues to be linked to the name Prażmowski.

PRAŻMOWSKI HOUSE

Situated at No. 87 Krakowskie Przedmieocie, this is the most beautiful such structure along the Royal Way. It is quite certain that J. Pastorius, the royal medic and historian, built it for himself in 1660 as the town was rebuilding in the wake of the Swedish invasion. In 1666 it became the property of Mikołaj Prażmowski who later became the Great Crown Chancellor and Primate of Poland, hence the building's accepted name. It got its palatial appearance after being rebuilt for the Leszczyńskis in 1754 -- a time when Saxon architects reigned supreme in Poland's capital. The rococo façade, with its decorative balconies and stone portal along its central axis, is accentuated by concave pilasters and crowned with cartouches cum putti.

ST ANN'S CHURCH

THE ADAM MICKIEWICZ MONUMENT

St Ann's Church, interior.

Built together with a Bernardine Monastery after 1454, it was founded by the Bolesław IV and his wife Anna, the Duke and Duchess of Masovia. It was rebuilt following the destruction suffered in 1660-1667. The classicist façade was built on in 1786-1788 after a design by Stanisław Kostka-Potocki and Christian Piotr Aigner and was funded by King Stanisław August, Duchess Izabela Czartoryska-Lubomirska and burgher Józef Kwiecinski. The church's rich baroque interior survived in 1944, although its roof did get destroyed in a blaze and the ceiling painting had to be recreated to restore its artistic integrity (Sławomira and Konstanty Tiunin). The survival of the church's interior was a remarkable occurrence, considering the nearly total destruction of the interior of other Warsaw churches. The monastery was abolished in 1864 as part of the Russians' reprisals for the anti-tsarist January Insurrection: It has served as the church of Warsaw University students since 1929.

This memorial, the work of Cyprian Godebski, was unveiled on 24 December 1898 on the 100th anniversary of the poet's birth. It was built through the free-will offerings of Polish society in appreciation for the patriotic role played by the bard's poetry. That aspect of his literary efforts was what promoted the Nazi occupiers to remove the statue in 1942. The head and a portion of the torso were retrieved, and the monument was restored for the benefit of Warsovians and Poles everywhere in 1950.

< A view of St Ann's Church. St Ann's Church as seen from Mariensztat.

Adam Mickiewicz Monument. >

Built in 1899-1901 at the corner of Krakowskie Przedmieocie and Karowa Street, it was Warsaw's biggest and most elegant hotel of its day. Construction was financed by a consortium created by Ignacy Paderewski, piano virtuoso and future prime minister of Poland. Designed by the most esteemed architect of that period, Władysław

Carmelite Church, interior.

Marconi, the six-storey building displays clear neo-renaissance and classicist traits, and extensive glassed-in surfaces adorn its lower two floors. In keeping with the consortium's intentions, in terms of size and rich decoration it eclipsed the Hotel Europejski on the opposite side of Krakowskie Przedmieocie. The interior décor of the lobby, dining-room, ballroom and suites was designed by Otto Wagner junior of Vienna. This was Warsaw's first large-scale manifestation of a new style -- the secession. Painter Wojciech Kossak had his atelier on the top floor. Since it was decided not to rebuild the houses standing between Karowa Street and Visitation Church, the Hotel Bristol has received a most favourable exposure. In the 1980s the building underwent modernisation and a contemporary floor was added.

CARMELITE CHURCH

After a wooden church had burnt down in 1656, it took nearly to the end of the century to build a brick one which was consecrated in 1701. The stone façade, designed by Efraim Szreger and funded by Michał and Karol Radziwiłł, was completed in 1782. Monumental classicism, balanced proportions and a high level of artistry in its details have made it an important architectural accent along this particular stretch of Krakowskie Przedmieście. The square in which the Adam Mickiewicz Monument stands heightens the church's towering hull. The square, created in the latter half of the 19th century by demolishing a string of townhouses, enhances the spatial values of this part of the Royal Way.

The church's late-baroque interior appointments were funded for the needs of the severe order of the Barefooted Carmelites. The order was abolished in 1864 as part of Russian reprisals for the January Insurrection.

Hotel Bristol.

THE PRESIDENTIAL PALACE AND J. PONIATOWSKI MONUMENT

MARSHAL JÓZEF PIŁSUDSKI MONUMENT

It had been variously known as Koniecpolski Palace, Radziwiłł Palace and the Viceroy's Palace, at present it is the seat of the President of Poland and houses his offices. The main hull was designed by Konstanty Tencalli and was built in c. 1643 for Grand Crown Hetman Stanisław Koniecpolski. After it had been owned for a time by the Lubomirskis, in the 18th century the Radziwiłłs contracted Antoni Solari to add a pair of wings (1738-1740) and modernise the palace's central core (1755-1759). The government of the Russian-controlled Kingdom of Poland bought the palace in 1817 and had Christian Piotr Aigner rebuild it. He modernised the elevation and interior in a classicist vein for the viceroy, General Józef Zajączek. In the 19th and 20th centuries the building was modernised and restored. The model of the equestrian monument of Józef Poniatowski, the work of Bertel Thorvaldsen, arose in 1826, having been commissioned by a civic committee. It was patterned on the ancient statue of Marcus Aurelius. It was cast in 1831, and Tsar Alexander I had it taken to Modlin Fortress, whereupon he presented it to his viceroy, Ivan Paksevich. In 1923 it was placed in Saxon Square, where it was destroyed in 1944. In 1951, the city of Copenhagen presented to Warsaw a copy of the statue cast from the original model. The monument has stood at its present site since 1965.

This monument, which stands at the head of Michał Tokarzewski-Karaszewicz Street, was unveiled in 1994. The bronze statue, designed by Tadeusz Łodziana, is set on a pro-portionately-sized syenite socle. Marshal Piłsudski is depicted engrossed in thoughts as he gazes in the direction of the Tomb of the Unknown So-ldier across the broad square bearing his name. Owing to the monument's modest sca-le, it is aptly situated. This, however, is probably not the ultimate form of paying tri-bute to a solider the nation associates with its regained independence in 1918 and its effective defence in 1920. Although there have been many contests for ways to architecturally develop all of Piłsudski Square, a satisfac-tory plan has yet to be created.

to a design by Karol Bay. The second stage was carried out by Efraim Szreger in 1754-1763. To him we owe the magnificent façade, with its slender columns and bas-reliefs created at the workshop of Jan Jerzy Plersch, as well as the rich interior in which late-baroque forms harmoniously intermingled with rococo elements. Schreger's main altar is adorned with a huge ebony tabernacle, endowed by Queen Ludwika Maria in c. 1655 and featuring silver plaquettes of great artistry. An original pulpit in the form of a symbolic ship was the work of the Plersch workshop (1762). Owing to its cloister status, the convent adjoining the church is not generally accessible. In the cloistered area a wooden, two-storey Calvary structure from the mid-18th century has survived. Accessible only to the nuns, it symbolises the durability of their tradition in the centre of a frequently-destroyed city. The church is an outstanding example of Polish baroque religious architecture. Its rank has been elevated by its interior's surviving artistic décor. But these elements do not dominate the beautifully-proportioned monumental interior architecture. The bright colour scheme of the main altar, notably its finials, remains subordinated to the architecture. The church's vibrant chiaroscuro-effect façade contrasts nicely with the compact, subdued form of the monument of Polish Primate Cardinal Stefan Wyszyński which stands out front. The work of A. Renes, it enriches the religious substance of the site, whilst constituting a contemporary artistic accent along the Royal Way.

CHURCH OF THE VISITATION SISTERS UNDER THE PROTECTION OF ST JOSEPH

The Sisters of the Visitation were brought from France by Queen Ludwika Maria Gonzaga in 1654. In the 18th century, the convent was taken into the care of Elżbieta Lubomirska-Sieniawska, a Grand Crown Hetman's wife known for her patronage of architecture and fine arts. She launched the first stage of the construction of the present church in 1728-1733 according

Pulpit.

Interior.

WARSAW UNIVERSITY

The campus covers a fair-sized area between Krakowskie Przedmieście and the slope of the Warsaw Escarpment. All its buildings have been listed in the registry of historical monuments and are under the constant care of conservators. Royal Warsaw University was established in 1816 through the merger of the School of Law and Administration and the School of Medicine. The principal animators of that move were Stanisław Kostka-Potocki and Father Stanisław Staszic. After its abolition in 1831, a Main School was established here in 1862. In 1869, it was transformed into Imperial Warsaw University with lectures delivered in Russian. Polonised after 1915, it was known simply as Warsaw University. Shut down in 1939, it was unable to function normally until 1945, so it went underground. Some 300 lecturers took part in the work of the clandestine university.

Kazimierz Palace, which now houses the offices of the rector and deans, was erect-

Kazimierz Palace.

Main Gate.

ed in 1634 under the endowment of King Władysław IV. It was done over in 1660 for King Jan Kazimierz, hence its name. Dominik Merlini adapted the palace for the use of the Cadet Corps, whose graduates included Tadeusz Kościuszko, the hero of two continents, and the well-known Polish writer Julian Ursyn Niemcewicz. The palace has a classicist façade featuring a towering colonnaded portico and a late-baroque elevation on the garden side.

Warsaw University Library, which stands in front of Kazimierz Palace, is a neo-renaissance structure built in 1891-1894 after a design by Stefan Szyller. It is soon due to be moved to a new building in Dobra Street not far from the Vistula. The campus's neo-baroque entrance gate was likewise designed by Szyller and erected in about 1900. An exceptional architectural work is Tyszkiewicz Palace, built by Jan Christian Kamsetzer (1786-1792) for Ludwika Tyszkiewicz, Grand Marshal of Lithuania. The classicist structure richly adorned with sculptures and stuccowork stands in Krakowskie Przedmieście. From 1840 to 1932 it was the property of the Potocki family. Nearly

a half of Warsaw University's buildings went up in smoke in 1939-1945 but were painstakingly restored after the war. The university's buildings are becoming increasingly cramped in view of the institution's ever-growing needs.

University Library.

es and elegant weddings. Such events led to the founding of altars, tombstones and works of art. Upon entering the upper church to find the 1880 monument of Fryderyk Chopin, one should recall that back in 1944 a bitter struggle was waged for the church and a cluster of missionary buildings. There wasn't a single art work that did not require conservation or reconstruction, although today that may be difficult to believe. Therein lies the greatness of this house of worship and its faithful who had lent a hand to its post-war reconstruction. That spirit of Warsovians was instrumental in having the Royal way entered in UNESCO's World Heritage List.

STASZIC PALACE

Father Stanisław Staszic (1755-1826) -- scholar, statesman, political activist, writer, patron of the arts and priest -- was greatly instrumental in organising and mapping the development of Polish arts and sciences. A member of the Society of Friends of Learning since 1800, he became its president in 1808 and built its seat in 1820-1824. He entrusted the palace's design to Antoni Corazzi, whom he had earlier brought to Poland. The occupation forces had the building's classicist elevation redone in a Byzantine-Russian style in 1892-1893 as part of a campaign to russify Warsaw's public buildings. Between the two World Wars, Marian Lalewicz to some extent restored the building's Corazzi heritage. Following a 1944 blaze, Piotr Bieganski fully recreated the building's classicist form (1947-1950). The traditional function of the building, originally erected as a centre of learning, has been maintained. It is now the seat of the Polish Academy of Science.

Behind the back of the Copernicus Monument, naturally also founded by Staszic, stands an historic palace which has risen from the ashes on four separate occasions over the past 124 years. That is what Warsaw is all about!

CHURCH OF THE FINDING OF THE CROSS

This two-storey church was designed by Józef Simon Bellotti and built in 1679-1696. The façade was created by Józef Fontana with the assistance of Joachim Daniel Jauch in 1725-1736 and completed in 1760 by Jakub Fontana. The monumental staircase above the entrance to the lower church was built in 1818. The statue of Christ carrying the cross, the work of Andrzej Pruszynski, was unveiled in 1858. A figure cast in bronze by Pius Welonski replaced the sculpted statue in 1898.

The superbly-situated twin-towered church with a monumental, albeit subdued façade dominates this stretch of Krakowskie Przedmieście. It owes its popularity to solemn memorial mass-

NOWY ŚWIAT STREET

The road from the ducal castle of Old Warsaw to Ujazdów Castle and further on to Czersk led along what today is Nowy Świat Street. In the 16th century, jurisdictions emerged in this area. These were rural areas excluded from the royal domain and subject only to rules established by their owners. The oldest one, named Nowoświecka (New World) Jurisdiction in 1539, in time became attached to the stretch of road between Krakowskie Przedmieście and Three-Crosses Square. Wooden structures dominated, but in the latter half of the 18th century seven palaces were built, including that of the Branickis and Sulkowskis. During the Kingdom of Poland period (1815-1831), 30 three-storey classicist townhouses were built, giving the street an architecturally uniform character. At the turn of the 19th to 20th centuries several taller townhouses were added, violating the scale of the architecture. Modernist accents also began appearing.

Only six of the 71 buildings survived the bitter fighting of the 1944 Warsaw Uprising. The basic premise of the post-war reconstruction effort was to revert to the scale of the Kingdom of Warsaw period. Most of the reconstruction projects were drawn up by Mieczysław Kuzma and Zygmunt Stępiński. In justified cases neutral façades were designed, but in keeping with the scale of their surroundings.

A townhouse complex representing the turn of the 19th to 20th centuries survived between Three-Crosses Square and Aleje Jerozolimskie. Reconstruction between Aleje Jerozolimskie and Krakowskie Przedmieście was completed in 1950.

Kossakowski Palace at No. 19 was built by Efraim Szreger c. 1755, and redone by Henryk Marconi in 1848-1849. Seriously damaged in 1939, it ceased to exist in 1944, but by 1949 reconstruction of the building's hull had been completed. Branicki Palace standing opposite was better preserved. It had been rebuilt in neo-renaissance form in the latter half of the 19th century according to a design by Henryk Marconi. Its right annexe still houses a popular chemist's shop known for its neo-gothic interior décor. The townhouse of Bishop Szczepan Hołowczyc at No. 35 was the work of Antoni Corazzi (1820), and was reconstructed in 1949 by Piotr Biegański who restored its classicist forms. The classicist house of Warsaw University Professor Feliks Bentkowski at No. 49 was the work of Hilary Szpilowski. More such townhouses and mansions have survived.

Gateways lead to the back of some of them where one may encounter a mini-shopping mall, an outdoor café or a lawn. Although the latest modernisation of 1995-1996 sparked off a heated polemic, it marked an attempt to improve the aesthetics and functionality of Warsaw's favourite promenade. A city lives only when it develops, modernises and adapts to the changing needs of its people. A good example of that is Nowy Świat, and what does not satisfy can always be changed. The only reasonable solution is to continue that process.

GNIŃSKI PALACE

Picturesequely perched on the edge of the Warsaw Escarpment, where Tamka Street begins its descent to the Vistula, this edifice dates from 1609. Duke Janusz Ostrogski, Castellan of Kraków had been planning to begin the construction of a fortified palace there. A remnant of that interrupted project is the brick bastion on which after 1681, according to plans drawn up by Tylman of Gameren, a building was erected for Crown Vice-Chancellor Jan Gniński as part of the future planned residence. Modernisation work at the site was conducted in 1719 for the Zamoyskis by Karol Bay. In 1820, Michał Gajewski bought the property from Chodkiewicz, the palace was elevated and subsequently served as a military field hospital. In 1859, the municipal authorities gave the building to the Institute of Music, the later Warsaw Conservatory. It went up in flame in 1944. Plans drawn up by Mieczysław Kuzma restored the beauty of its hull and of its richly stucco-adorned interior. Since 1953 it has been the world-renowned seat of the Fryderyk Chopin Society. A popular legend is associated with the bastion. A young cobbler from Old Town sneaked into the bastion's cellar and received 100 thalers from the golden duck living there, promising to spend them all by midnight in order to win a splendid prize. He returned convinced that he had accomplished his task, not knowing that two tiny coins had fallen out of his pocket. He had not fulfilled the conditions, hence he could not be rewarded.

ST ALEKSANDER'S CHURCH AND THREE-CROSSES SQUARE

In the years from 1724 to 1731 King August II Wettin established a Way of the Cross leading south from the area of what is now Three-Crosses Square. Two columns crowned with gilded crosses have survived. The third cross adorns the dome of the church, hence the square's name.

The size and architecture of the square have been repeatedly corrected. A total of nine streets converge on the square, making it the only one of its kind in Warsaw. Its area was considerably expanded in 1815. It was named Alexander Square when Warsaw became the capital of the Russian-controlled Kingdom of Poland. A triumphal arch was erected in the square to welcome Tsar Alexander I, who also had the title 'King of Poland' and had come on a visit from his capital of St Petersburg. From, 1818 to 1825 the church of St Aleksander was built there according to a design developed by Chrystian Piotr Aigner.

In the period from 1886 to 1894, when a governor-general resided in Warsaw, then the capital of a Russian province called Vistulaland, the church was done over in the neo-renaissance style, creating a edifice alien to the town's spirit. Following its extensive damage in 1944, its original classicist form was restored by Stanisław Marzyński (1947-1958), an architect of great merit for Warsaw's churches.

The church's shapely classicist hull, with its two six-column porticoes, dome and lower church in the basement, has again become the square's dominant feature. But not many elements from the immediate vicinity have survived. Contemporary buildings have filled the war-caused gaps, attesting to the city's vitality. In effect, the square has become a living chronicle of the past half a century of passing fashions in architectural design. But not all the newer buildings have met with public approval. It should be pointed out that the square's final architectural composition has yet to be completed, and that places high requirements on investors and designers alike, especially as regards the south end of the square.

The following incident characterstic of the 1970s has now all but been forgotten. Protests were sparked off by a plan to remove an open-air pissoir -- 'the last such unique vestige of Old Warsaw', as opponents of the move argued.

UJAZDÓW CASTLE

This structure has a beautiful history -- and one typical of Warsaw. On the site of a former ducal castle-town a hunting lodge was built. In the 16th century, Anna Jagiellonian resided there and expanded the property. In 1578, the lodge was the scene of the first performance of 'Dismissal of the Greek Envoys' by Jan Kochanowski. The play was staged to add splendour to the wedding fête of Grand Crown Chancellor Jan Zamoyski and Krystyna Radziwiłł. Zygmunt III Vasa had a square castle with four corner towers built on the site. Later architect Tylman of Gameren did his part. King August II Wettin had the Piaseczno Canal dug near the castle. King Stanisław August Poniatowski gave the building to the city of Warsaw (1784). From 1810 it served as a military hospital, and pavilions for the sick were built on. It received wounded defenders of Warsaw in 1939. Like so many Warsaw buildings, Ujazdów Castle went up in flames during the 1944 Warsaw Uprising. The state authorities ordered what was left of it to be dismantled (1954), causing then city conservator Piotr Biegański to resign in protest. The castle was rebuilt in the 1970s according to Biegański's design, and from 1981 it has housed the Centre of contemporary Art. Readers may be surprised by the fact that the ruins were completely dismantled, only to have the castle reconstructed a quarter of a century later.

That is what happens when state authorities directly run things, shunting experts onto the sidelines. It is good when an expert displays strength of character. Hence it is commendable that the castle's reconstruction was entrusted to the one who once had to resign in view of the authorities' power and arrogance. That also is Warsaw!

FRYDERYK CHOPIN MONUMENT

The Fryderyk Chopin Monument was unveiled in the section of Łazienki Park that adjoins Aleje Ujazdowskie (Ujazdów Avenue). It portrays the composer sitting transfixed as he listens to the rustling of a stylised willow-tree. The model created by Wacław Szymanowski (1904) was cast in bronze and represents stylistic traits of the Secession period.

The design had already been approved in 1909 but the outbreak of the World War and subsequent obstacles postponed the unveiling. The work appealed neither to the critics nor the public. But when the German occupiers destroyed the monument in 1940, Warsovians felt the lack of the image of Chopin, whose Revolutionary Étude, polonaises and mazurkas had accompanied them during those difficult years and helped to keep their patriotic feelings alive. The reconstructed monument was unveiled in 1958. Music-lovers attending outdoor summer concerts at the base of the monument can hear Polish and foreign virtuosos paying tribute to the Great Fryderyk. Perhaps some may wonder why this sculpture once did not speak to the people of Warsaw.

BELWEDER

Krzysztof Pac, Grand Chancellor of Lithuania, in 1659 built his suburban villa on this site. Situated at the edge of the escarpment with a broad, picturesque view of the Vistula, it was called Belweder. ('Belvedere' in Italian means beautiful view.) When it became the property of the Lubomirskis, another storey was added and a couple of wings were built on, creating a forecourt. In 1767, Stanisław August bought the palace together with the grounds of today's Łazienki Park and had a faience factory set up there. In 1818, the government of the Russian-controlled Kingdom of Poland purchased the property. It commissioned Jakub Kubicki, a disciple of D. Merlini, to modernise the entire building as a residence for Prince Konstanty Pavlovich, the brother of Tsar Alexander I, the constitutional king of the Russian-held part of Poland. The modest but shapely palace, with its colonnaded potricoes on both sides (1819-1822), is a classicist building. Its interior has survived although the wings have been repeatedly done over. The Belweder made history on the night of 29 November 1830, when Polish conspirators sought to assassinate the hated tsarist viceroy of the Kingdom of Poland. From 1918 to 1922 it was the residence of Marshal Józef Piłsudski, the Head of State. From 1922 to 1926 it served as the residence of Polish Presidents Gabriel Narutowicz and Stanisław Wojciechowski. From 1926 until his death on 12 May 1935 Józef Piłsudski lived in the Belweder, and up till 1939 it was a museum to his memory. President Lech Walesa lived there after he was elected, but later moved to the Presidential Palace. Inside is an exhibition titled 'Józef Piłsudski - Marshal of Poland'.

View from the east.

Raspberry Room.

ROYAL
ŁAZIENKI

THE WATER
PALACE

An exceptional corner of Warsaw this is, where for more than two centuries history has graciously protected against the vandalism of victors (save for two exceptions in 1940-1941). This palace-and-garden complex began taking shape in the latter half of the 17th century. Since then, the metropolis has greatly expanded to where Royal Łazienki is almost in the city-centre. This complex's beautiful name (which means 'the Royal Baths' in Polish) was popularised and made a household word by Marek Kwiatkowski, the park's custodian from 1960 and now

its director -- a man of limitless energy and unswerving devotion to his job.

In the latter half of the 17th century, Grand Crown Marshal Stanisław Herakliusz Lubomirski began to build recreational structures in the extensive, forested areas of the former Ujazdów game park (where the Dukes of Masovia used to hunt). Royal architect Tylman of Gameren on a tiny islet built a bath pavilion (1683-1690). Even before being elected king Stanisław August Poniatowski bought the property. Involved as he was with repairs and alterations at the Royal Castle, he did not set about redoing Łazienki (the Baths) until 1770, which were designed and constructed over the next 20 years by Domenico Merlini. He had at his disposal the finest artists under the king's patronage. As a sign of the esteem he harboured for the work of his renowned predecessor, he preserved nearly all of Tylman's baroque-style interior divisions. The southern elevation, with its four-column niche accentuating the entrance, as seene from the

broad terrace, incorporates a baroque-style composition. What is more, in the arcade beyond the columns a portion of the old façade, with the main portral set in a break, has survived. The entire interior arrangement is harmonious and functional. The grand ballroom in the left wing marks the building's shorter side and widens the former Lubomirski Bathroom. The interior's wealth of classicist stucco and painted décor allow one to clearly distinguish four stages of this exceptional baroque-classicist composition. So as not to force Readers to launch personal research into various styles, it should be stated that the baroque has been preserved in the ante room, Bachus' Chamber and the Bathroom.

The classicist hull of the Water Palace is crowned by a prominent entablature with an open-work attic, embellished with statues set on socles. Similar in character are the two wings set on land and joined to the main body of the palace by arcaded bridges featuring colonnades with entablature and attic. This is an outstanding work of architecture, small in scale but not devoid of monumentalism. Thanks to the extensive statuary adorning its elevations and the area in front of them, the palace does not display the stiff and cold characteristics typical of the architecture of that period. It suffices to compare Merlini's contemporary work in Łazienki Park - the Myślewicki Palace (1775-1784), or Jakub Kubicki's Belweder (1819-1822) which now is part of the Łazienki complex. It can be assumed that King Stanisław August himself exerted considerable influence on the development of the architecture and its individual details. He had the habit of maintaining working contacts with his artists, and he gave his suburban residence his own personal touch. In particular, he revealed his personal participation in shaping the Round Hall. It has retained the dimensions given it by his predecessor, but the interior was endowed with an entirely new ideative and artistic character. It became a pantheon of Poland's reigning monarchs. In individual niches stand sculptures depicting Casimir the Great, Zygmunt the Old, Stefan Batory and John III Sobieski, whom Stanisław August esteemed

Gallery at the palace. >

the most. Over the doorway were the busts of Roman emperors Trajan, Titus and Marcus Aurelius. They were the work of Jakub Monaldi, Andrzej Le Brun and Franciszek Pinck. In the cupola are the circular paintings of Marcelo Bacciarelli personifying the virtues of Courage (depicted with the visage

North elevation.

Finial fragment.

Ball-room.

of King Stanisław August), Justice, Prudence and Goodness. As at the Royal Castle, the place of official visits, also in this country residence the king wished to remind visitors that they were guests of the majestic Polish Commonwealth. He did not get to admire the completed work, being as he was in far-away St Petersburg, where he was taken after the third and final partition of Poland.

Solomon's Hall.

In 1944, the German occupiers drenched the interior of the Water Palace with petrol and set fire to it. They also drilled about 1,000 holes in its walls in order to blow it up as they had the Royal Castle. Architect Jan Dąbrowski drew up plans to restore the building and supervised the project which was launched immediately after liberation. Since 1960 curator Marek Kwiatkowski has not only been in charge of everything but has also organised evenings of chamber music or poetry by candle-light as well as festive gatherings of various bodies. The visitors that come here are his guests, although they remain under the spell of this place so beloved and permeated by the spirit of Stanisław August Poniatowski.

Statue of Diana.

Rotunda. >

THE WHITE HOUSE

This was the earliest Łazienki structure (1774-1777) built as part of the king's programme to create a suburban royal residence. The prolonged work on the reconstruction and expansion of the Lubomirski Baths and the creation of the Water Palace determined the function of the White House as the personal seat of Stanisław August. Merlini designed the modest, square, two-floor, building with identical rusticated elevations and a belvedere on the roof. Most of its rooms have retained their

< Łazienki Park.

original character and décor. Here one may fully appreciate the grotesque paintings of Bogumił Plersch. The dining-room was adorned with frescoes alluding to the then fashionable compositions of the Vatican's Raphaelite Loggias. Here they symbolised the four elements: Water, Air, Fire and Earth as well as Day and Night. The patterned floor underscored the lightness of

Breakfast room.

Plersch's work. The ancient statue of Venus Anadyomene was most likely purchased for the king in Rome (1777) for the express purpose of filling the dining-room niche, where it is found today. Owing to the whiteness of its marble and the fact that it is set back -- it does not constitute a prominent accent disrupting the room's painted composition. The entire room together with its appointments is a well-considered, collective work of art. The modest architectural shape of the White House contrasts with the wealth and lightness of the royal chambers found in its interior. One may assume that that was the intended effect, in order to make all the bigger impression on guests of the Water Palace. The structure is situated between the Royal Promenade and the main lane leading to the Water Palace complex, where the landscaping already suggests a romantic park.

AMPHITHEATRE - ISLET THEATRE

The amphitheatre was built at the edge of the Royal Pond in 1775-1778 according to a design by Jan Chrystian Kamsetzer. The audience seated there watches the activities on a stage replete with stylised ancient ruins and set on a tiny islet. The entire arrangement is popularly referred to as the Islet Theatre. It is a classicist composition. The crown of the amphitheatre is rimmed with statues of ancient poets sculpted by Tomasz Righi according to the designs of Andrzej Le Brun. Beneath the arcades at the foot of the stricture is a café. The amphitheatre performs many functions as the scene of concerts by ensembles and soloists and even of fashion shows, but that does not violate the national character of the historical monument known as Royal Łazienki. When performances are not taking place, the amphitheatre is an ideal place to rest away from the beaten promenades. The peace, quiet and serene setting have a tranquillising effect just as they did in King Stanisław August's day.

In 1997, the Islet Theatre's stylised ruins underwent a general renovation, as did the actors' dressing-rooms and the entire amphitheatre.

THE NEW ORANGERIE

This structure is situated in the south end of Łazienki along the Chinese Road. It was designed by Warsaw University graduate Adolf Adam Loewe before he left for further studies abroad.It was erected in 1860-1861 to accommodate plants from the Old Orangerie, which was then nearly 100 years old and was housed in the Royal Theatre. Contemporary post-modernist architecture with its glassed halls seems a throw-back to such structures. The idea to expand the New Orangerie's garden function to include an elegant restaurant was a good innovation. The building's setting and the abundant verdure gracing its interior create an ideal atmosphere for culinary adventures.

The Palaces's garden elevation.

PALACE
IN WILANÓW

In the third year of his reign (1677), King John III Sobieski became sufficiently acquainted with Warsaw and its environs to purchase the village of Milanów as the site of planned royal residence and changed its name to Wilanów. There he found the foundation of a building whose construction had been started by Grand Vice-Chancellor Bogusław Leszczyński. Augustyn Locci began by building a brick, ground-floor Old Polish-style manorhouse with recessed corners. But already in 1681-1683 a mezzanine was added, and side galleries with corner towers were built on in front. In 1692, the building's residential core was elevated, the towers were topped with baroque helmets incorporating figures of Atlas, the façades of the galleries were embellished with attics and the entire structure started resembling a palace.

Modernisation projects initiated by successive owners of Wilanów expanded the structure without obliterating the

distinguishing features of Sobieski's palace. It continues to be adorned by battle scenes created on stuccowork panels by Stefan Szwaner, stone sculptures of the Muses and busts of Roman emperors, with copper and gilded helmets accentuating the building's core, founded by the king. The palace's artistic message -- singing the praises of the victorious monarch -- has remained intact thanks to the efforts of conservators.

Subsequent owners of the palace -- although they were not crowned heads -- did not damage the composition created and enriched by John III. The property was owned by the Sieniawskis, Czartoryskis, Potockis, Branickis and (since 1945) the National Museum in Warsaw.

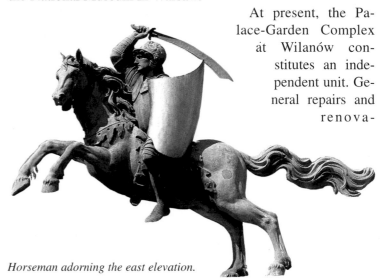

At present, the Palace-Garden Complex at Wilanów constitutes an independent unit. General repairs and renova-

Horseman adorning the east elevation.

tions were carried out in the palace from 1955 to 1965 under the supervision of Stefan Deubel and Jacek Cydzik. All of the walls and constructions were reinforced, and wall paintings, stuccowork and external stone sculptures underwent renovation. Facilities for sight-seers were improved. In the south wing, an entrance leads to a new basement, in which a cloak-room and waiting-room have been created for the benefit of visitors. A new staircase has made it possible to better manage individual visitors and tourist groups. Air-conditioning has also been installed. A superb Polish portrait gallery has been set up in the lofts, thereby enshrining modern times in the annals of the palace. Conservation work at Wilanów is conducted on a per-

Saturn's sun-dial.

< Wilanów Palace, east elevation.

Wilanów Palace, east elevation. >

The Queen's bed-chamber.

manent basis.

Wilanów Palace is the most important part of this large complex comprising various buildings and a spacious park. The gardens directly adjacent to the palace have had their baroque flavour restored according to plans drawn up by Gerard Ciołek. A grand staircase leads from its east side down to a lower level situated on Lake Wilanów. To the north stretches the Anglo - Chinese

Plafond in the Royal Study.

section of the park, laid out in 1784-1791 by Szymon Zug. Only a stroll through the park -- an attempt to absorb its scale and variegated landscaping principles, its vistas, reflecting pools, statuary and buildings of various size -- enables one to comprehend what is meant by the term palace-garden 'complex'. In fact, that assignment can be best accomplished by spacing it out over several successive visits to Wilanów. It should also be borne in mind that parks and gardens were not set up for sightseers but as a place to commune with nature, a place of relaxation, recreation and contemplation. Only with such a frame of mind can one fully benefit from the gifts of nature which the owners of the gardens and parks, architects, gardeners and passing generations, engaged in upholding these values for centuries, have created for themselves and posterity.

Of course, the most important section of the palace are the royal suites, once used by John III and his family. They have retained intact their scale and functional connecting passageways designed by Augustyn Locci according to the king's wish-

es.

Researchers have called attention to the fact that the palace's building plan clearly resembles that of an Old Polish manor-house. That came to be as a result of the king's will, not at the suggestion of his gifted Italian architect. He had been summoned there to implement the task commissioned by the monarch. The term 'little Versailles', often repeated by foreign visitors, is both inaccurate and misleading. John III launched the construction of his suburban villa, when work on the palace in Versailles (from 1661) had been quite advanced. The resources the king of France had at his disposal ensure the implementation of his project on a spatial and artistic scale which no-one could match. Sobieski governed a state no smaller than France (excluding its overseas dominions), but in his country he set forth and implemented a different set of priorities. He had no reason to compete in the architectural realm, as victorious battles constituted his claim to greatness. Although both palaces start with a 'v' sound, Versailles and Wilanów are two separate phenomena that defy comparison.

Three centuries after the Wilanów interior had been furnished and decorated it would be difficult to expect intact and complete compositions. Nevertheless, not only does the residence's family-home atmosphere surprise one -- so does the wealth of original baroque works and, even more importantly, the fact that many of them were directly connected with the king. 'Those visiting these chambers are guests of His Majesty himself,' is what Wojciech Fijałkowski used to say. He was the curator of the palace during the great renovation and interior arrangement that has ensured the palace a place among the world's leading palatial residences.

The position of Wilanów has also been enhanced by the Poster Museum. During the renovation of the palace's out-

Royal ante-chamber.

buildings, a small, new, modern building was erected behind the façade of the old coach-house to house the collection. It was designed by Halina Kossuth, Jacek Cydzik and Adam Pulikowski. The museum has become the venue of a biennial exhibition of contemporary posters which has gained international rank. Wilanów has become a meeting-place for the world's most outstanding artists, a centre which attracts them from America, Japan and Australia.

The palace-park complex does not end at the boundaries of the former royal residence. Some of its most important structures and areas, developed under royal patronage, are situated beyond the fort and stone gate accentuating the main entrance (erected in 1689 and decorated in the 18th century). There are also a number of buildings beyond the palatial grounds which are referred to as palace-related. Their character has changed over the years as they were modernised or expanded by successive owners or users. Some of them are no longer functionally connected to the servicing of the palace-park complex, although they are significant to the palace-oriented locality of Wilanów. One cannot overlook the patronage of the Potockis who during the 19th century erected or

Royal bed-chamber.

redid auxiliary buildings accompanying the complex. Mention should be made of St Ann's Hospital and the Doctor's House at 6 Biedronki Street. All of them have been subordinated to the character of this place, to the module of its architecture. Even the old Wilanów railway station was erected by Konstanty Jakimowicz in 1920 in a manor-house.

Chinese gazebo in the park >

Holiday Inn Hotel.

CITY-CENTRE

The neighbouring photo may be viewed from two totally different standpoints. This monumental structure with a capacity of 800,000 cubic metres houses scores of important institutions (offices of the Polish Academy of Science, the Goethe Institute, the Polish UNESCO Committee, a Museum of Technology, theatres and..... even a gambling casino) and is nicely integrated with Warsaw's transport network. Seen at the bottom of the illustration is the convenient entrance to the tunnel beneath Marszałkowska Street as well as department stores with a shopping mall. But one may also view the structure as a symbol of evil domination -- and a huge one at that, soaring to a height of 230 metres (minus the television spire), which should be razed as soon as possible because..... And the once state-owned department stores are relics of the tradition of central goods distribution and an unreal economy. Nearly everything written above is true, and that truth is situated in the very centre of central Warsaw. Existence is a trait of matter that is beyond discussion.

< *Palace of Culture.*

In the past, urban-development plans had been created for entire neighbourhoods including the centre. Approved by the proper bureaucratic bodies, they became law, and municipal ownership of property and financial resources from the budget were its tools of enforcement. Today planning also takes place, but the era of arbitrary and all-powerful town planners is now only a memory. The determining factors are the right of ownership and the investor's real financial reserves. For that reason, the underground as well as surface-level traffic and transport arrangements are emer-

Hotel Forum.

Dmowski Circle.

ging with such difficulty.

In 1996, a competition for a Warsaw town-planning scheme was resolved (it was won by the team of Zygmunt Ziobrowski of Kraków). At the same time the firm Dom i Miasto (Home and Town) published a fascinating illustration titled 'New Ideas for Warsaw', based on an original town-planning study. Thus two sets of urban-development concepts, backed by studies, were born. A year has passed but that is no cause for impatience in anticipation of general decisions. They can be announced, after all, only when negotiations with the investors of individual tasks have been completed. A significant problem in Warsaw is the difficulty in establishing property rights.

One should therefore not be concerned that a tall, brown-coloured office tower, whose lower wing juts deep into Prosta Street, now stands at Rondo ONZ (UN Circle), whilst the circle's easterly Świętokrzyska Street side remains overgrown with grass. We are in a period when war-time gaps as well as providentially set-aside land reserves are being filled in, and Warsaw has become an Eldorado for builders. In the near future, unemployment poses no threat to the Warsaw Metropolis, since each new building means dozens if not hundreds of new jobs. Are there justifiable fears that architecturally less fortunate if not downright ugly buildings will rise? Indeed there are, because du-

Hotel Mercure.

ring negotiations with investors the power of persuasion of the architectural and building authorities are rather limited. As in the arts, so too in the realm of architectural design not all creations are outstanding, and that is how things have always been. However, the big opportunity of the present period of architectural development is the ability to meet the ambitious demands of investors and creative architects. One need not fear the still not fully-mastered principles of a free urban game which bold, experienced architects are encouraging. Our present opening on world design trends is sure to bring about provocative works alien to our aesthetic views. At this point it might be appropriate to mention the nick-names Warsaw's man-in-the-street has coined for certain buildings: Cornerless Place, At the Sign of the Toilet-seat, At the Sign of the Bra and Daft House. These names are at once sarcastic and affectionate. These buildings continue to serve and only occasionally does someone recall their old nick-names. The city is able to live with strange and criticised architecture. Everyone can have pimples, especially during a rapid drive to maturity.

The biggest threat to the city-centre are construction projects that eliminate green areas. Every cut-down tree, every square metre of lawn replaced by an artificial car-park surface, transport facility or building means the irreversible limiting of social space. That term is applied to recreation areas where natural, people-friendly expanses foster inter-personal contacts. In this realm, both architectural officials as well as representatives of Warsaw's neighbourhood councils have yet to come up with a long-range view into the future. Warsaw's beloved pre-war Mayor Stefan Starzyński had put into practice the slogan of 'Warsaw in flowers'. The generation of the great post-war reconstruction introduced extensive green areas into central Warsaw. The creation of green strips paralleling the East-West Route from the Vistula almost as far as Bank Square has been regarded over the past half a century as an achievement of European-wide significance. The concept of liquidating the green area between Świętokrzyska Street and the Palace of Culture, attempts to build things along the edges of Saxon Garden and the liquidation of gardens in Żoliborz, which has been under way for several years now, foretells a general attack on the achievements of several generations.

Aleje Jerozolimskie.

Ilmet Tower.

City-Centre. >

GREAT THEATRE

Built in 1825-1833 according to plans drawn up by Antoni Corazzi, the Great Theatre features decorative sculptures by Tomasz Accardi, Konstanty Hegel and Paweł Maliński. The left wing of the theatre was formerly a building known as Under the Columns, designed by Christian Piotr Aigner. The right wing was designed as a ball room by Corazzi. The driveway portico was added in 1890. The name 'Great Theatre' caught on in about 1840, as did the name 'Theatre Square'. The building was burnt down in 1939, its ruins were blown up in 1944 and only its classicist colonnaded façade was spared. The building was rebuilt from 1951 to 1965 according to the plans of Borden Pniewski, and its capacity increased considerably. The monuments of Wojciech Bogusławski and Stanisław Moniuszko were the work of Jan Szczepkowski. The artist unveiled the first, a bronze statue of the 'father' of the Polish theatre on a characteristic socle adorned with figures, in 1936. In 1944 only the socle had survived, so a replica was created and placed on it. The statue of the outstanding Polish composer Moniuszko was unveiled together with its socle in 1965.

FINANCIAL CENTRE IN BANKOWY SQUARE

In 1773-1785, Jakub Fontana designed a late-baroque palace for Adam Jabłonowski, Voivod of Great Poland. It was soon sold, and in 1816 it was purchased by the municipal authorities and adapted for use as a town-hall. Burnt during the January Insurrection, from 1864 to 1869 it was rebuilt and considerably expanded inwardly by J. Orłowski. At that time, the roof-line was elevated and a fire-tower was moved from the rear of the building to its façade. The new form of the partitioner's town-hall dominated the square. In 1939, it was from there that Warsaw's heroic Mayor Stefan Starzyński guided the city's defence. The building was burnt in 1944 and what was left of it was removed in 1952. The Monument to the Heroes of Warsaw, designed by Marian Konieczny and popularly known as the Warsaw Nike, was set up in 1964 in the empty plaza.

In order to restore the former closed composition of Theatre Square, an offer to build a financial centre at the site was accepted. The result is a modern building hidden behind a curtain wall simulating the 1863 façade, created after Polish insurgents had

set fire to the town-hall. Whether it was worth building so prominent an edifice, dominating the colonnade of the Great Theatre, is a question not worth asking after the fact. But one should not use such names as 'Jabłonowski Palace' or 'old town-hall' to designate the modern financial centre. The most slighted of all was the neighbouring Blank Palace -- a true palace. In an effort to improve its surroundings and exposure, the house standing opposite in Nowy Przejazd Street was lowered. Amid all those strange changes, the Warsaw Nike was given superior artistic and spatial exposure. Set on a taller socle than previously against a more ordered landscape, the monument's force of expression has been emphasised.

Warsaw Nike.

Financial Centre.

WARSAW NIKE

Unveiled in Theatre Square in 1964 on the site of the former town hall, it was the work of Marian Konieczny, who had won a competition for the best design in 1959. The sculpture symbolises an Undefeated City, as Warsaw has been traditionally called. The decision to restore Theatre Square's traditional character of an integral urban composition, was necessitated by the transfer of the monument to another site. Its present location, at the point where Nowy Zjazd Street flows into Aleja Solidarności (Solidarity Avenue), combines with its taller socle to give the monument more dramatic expression and superior exposure.

Palace of the Commission of Revenue and Treasury.

BANK SQUARE

Now probably the busiest Warsaw square, it began taking shape in 1852, when Antoni Corazzi undertook the task of building the financial centre of the Russian-controlled Kingdom of Poland, comprising three classicist structures. Those buildings have the address of 1, 3 and 5 Bank Square. In 1825-1828 at the corner of Elektoralna Street a two-floor building topped with a copula was built to house the Bourse and Bank of Poland. At present it houses the John Paul II Gallery, entered from Elektoralna Street. The next is the 17th-century Wiśniowiecki Palace, later known as the Ogiński Palace. From 1825 to 1830 it was redone to serve as the residence of Treasury Minister Franciszek Ksawery Drucki-Lubecki, and now it contains the offices of the City of Warsaw authorities. The three-floor building at No. 5 with its richly-diversified architecture was once the Palace of Government Revenue and Treasury. Earlier it had belonged to Jan Leszczyński, Józef Potocki and the Zielińskis. At present it is the Office of the Warsaw Voivod. It was rebuilt in 1823-1825 to become a three-floor building with a forecourt. The decorative sculptures were the work of Paweł Maliński and M. Vincenti.

Destroyed in the 1944 conflagration, the palaces were rebuilt according to plans developed by Piotr Biegański. In 1951, the square was given its present rectangular shape to include an extension of Marszałkowska Street, which was widened after flowing in from Saxon Garden into the square. At the corner of Aleja Solidarności a skyscraper, now known as the blue office tower, was built from 1975 to 1992. At its base stands a barely visible monument to Warsaw Mayor Stefan Starzyński, which was unveiled in 1993.

Stefan Starzyński Monument.

< *Blue Tower.*

Garden elevation of Krasiński Palace.

KRASIŃSKI PALACE

Tympanum of the main elevation.

< Saxon Garden.

The most beautiful of Warsaw's palaces stands in Krasiński Square. It was built in 1677-1683 for Jan Dobrogost Krasiński, starost of Warsaw and later voivod of Płock. It was the work of Tylman of Gameren in co-operation with J. Belotti, J. Solari and I. Affaita. An extended, three-floor palace with corner recesses and a central recess in both the front and garden façades, its style has been referred to as classicist baroque. The triangular fields of the great pediments of the central recesses are filled with well-developed relief compositions apotheosising the House of Krasiński. They were the work of Andreas Schülter, then Poland's most outstanding sculptor. In 1756, the palace was purchased to serve as the seat of the Commonwealth Treasury Commission and Crown Registry. Hence the proud name 'Palace of the Commonwealth' is used interchangeably with that of its original founder. During the period between the two World Wars, it housed the Supreme Court. That necessitated the construction of an additional complex of Supreme Court buildings on the east and north side of the palace. Destroyed in a blaze in 1939, its was rebuilt in the years 1948 to 1961 according to plans which Mieczysław Kuzma and Zygmunt Stepinski drew up on the basis of the palace's late-18th-century appearance. At present the building houses the Special Collections of Poland's National Library. This was the first attempt on such a scale to recreate the composition of venerable old square by combining contemporary architectural forms with those of a

bygone era. It commands respect and hopefully can show the advocates of reconstruction that the contemporary age has a right to conduct a friendly dialogue with history.

ZACHĘTA GALLERY

In 1860, a Society for the Encouragement of Fine Arts was established. ('Zachęta' is the Polish word for 'encouragement'.) Its founding members included Wojciech Gerson, Jerzy Kossak and Jan Ignacy Kraszewski. From 1899 to 1903 in Małachowski Square, a monumental edifice designed by Stefan Szyller was erected as the seat of the Society with exhibition halls. The neobaroque structure with a colonnaded portico and rich decorative sculptures has been in the service of national culture ever since. It was here that Poland's first president, Gabriel Narutowicz, was assassinated on 16 December 1922. Zachęta's halls regularly play host to national, international and monographic exhibitions. In 1990, the society resumed its activities as the Society for the Encouragement of Fine Arts at Zachęta Gallery.

TOMB OF THE UNKNOWN SOLDIER

It is situated in Marsha3 Piłsudski Square beneath the three arcades of a connector built for Ivan Skvartsov (1832-1842) to join the wings of Saxon Palace. The Tomb of the Unknown Solider was designed by S. Ostrowski, and the remains of an Unknown Soldier together with the soil from different battlefields enshrined, in 1925. All that was left of the palace, destroyed in 1944, were the arcades and column fragments. The ruins underwent repairs, the decorations were enhanced (H. Grunwald) and the names of new battle-fields were added. The latter activity was repeated in 1988-1991. This place of national memory, watched over by a permanent guard of honour, is the scene of the most important national and state ceremonies. Despite numerous attempts, no decision has been taken as to how to develop the surroundings of the Tomb.

Panorama of Warsaw. >

URB.
Sedes O
Poloniæ e
spiciebat
à Ser. R
Sueciæ
fuil

Donus Venatoria   Villa Regia   Sacellum Moscovitarum   Palatium Conietopolskianum   Palatium Ossolinskianum   Palatium Radzieiowskianum   Templum Bernhar dinorum   Regis ... ... Sueciæ

Gynæcium   Templum Carmelitarum   Suburbia causta

Camth moad Callinarum

Redutus Venustate collaqens

V I S   T V L A